TOBACCO & FLUORIDE:

TWO ESSAYS ON DOMESTIC AND INTERNATIONAL PUBLIC HEALTH POLICY

MATTHEW HOWARD

2015

Paperback ISBN-10: 0692460047
Paperback ISBN-13: 978-0692460047
Kindle Ebook ASIN: B00Z00IF2U

Contents

Introduction

Consider two substances, each with a body of research confirming its toxicity to human beings. People consume one of the substances for pleasure, and the other for its supposed health benefits. The World Health Organization actively bands nations together to reduce the marketability and consumption of the former, yet promotes the latter as an effective health measure. The essays in this book examine the policies governing these two substances: tobacco and fluoride.

Tobacco control policies have gained significant traction as nations around the world evaluate the success of Australia's recent laws concerning cigarette packaging. Given impetus by the World Health Organization's *Framework Convention on Tobacco Control*, these policies have met with little public resistance, their sole opponents being the companies which manufacture tobacco products.

At the same time, another movement has gained traction: the opposition to adding fluoride to municipal water systems. Though the World Health Organization advocates fluoridation, a growing number of researchers and voters have called its touted benefits into question. Unlike tobacco, the efforts to eliminate fluoride have met resistance from the medical establishment.

What is the future of these two substances, each known to have harmful effects on human beings and yet viewed so differently in the court of public opinion? The two essays in this book will answer that question. Thank you for reading.

Matthew Howard
June 2015

Leading the Pack:

Australia's Plain Packaging Laws and Tobacco Control Measures Define the Growing International Conflict between Public Health Policy and Intellectual Property Rights

I. Introduction.

The global response to Australia's tobacco control measures reveals the complexity of international politics where trade agreements about intellectual property come into conflict with public health policy. The Australian measures taken to fulfill its commitment as a signatory party to the World Health Organization's Framework Convention on Tobacco Control gave tobacco companies occasion to sue the federal government for infringement on their brands. As more and more FCTC signatory countries begin to adopt measures like Australia's, tobacco companies and nations where they have major operations have brought disputes to the World Trade Organization. Certain trade restrictions brought about in the name of public health, they claim, violate various articles of TRIPS, the international agreement on Trade Related aspects of Intellectual Property Rights. The outcome of these disputes remains to be seen, with the World Trade Organization expecting to issue a decision on a major dispute in 2016. However, Australia's highest federal courts have supported these measures and denied claims to tobacco companies. It comes as little surprise, since these measures originated from advocates at the federal level from nations federally committed to the Framework Convention on Tobacco Control. Will the World Trade

Organization similarly uphold tobacco control policies at the international level?

This essay will review the political and judicial history of the Australian tobacco control measures, specifically with regards to "plain packaging" laws but including related measures of their comprehensive policies. This paper will highlight the strong support for the effectiveness of Australia's measures by the national and international research teams publishing analytical evaluations of them. The effects these measures have had on other nations include a wave of trade agreement disputes, but the United Kingdom's recent adoption of similar plain packaging laws scheduled to take effect in 2016 suggests a confidence the World Trade Organization will not be an unconquerable obstacle to the wave of nations fulfilling their commitments to the Framework Convention on Tobacco Control and radically changing the face of tobacco sales around the world.

II. Origins of Australia's Plain Packaging Laws.

Three years ago, the BBC News reported on "new" restrictions on cigarette packaging in Australia. Packs of cigarettes, they revealed, would come in a drab, dark brown color without any tobacco company logos or colors. The Australian federal government set this public health policy as part of a larger effort to reduce the number of smokers in their country to less than 10 percent by 2018 (Kennedy, 2012). But the story of the graphic health warnings and drab brown packaging now sold in Australia at a heavily taxed price go back to 2003, when the World Health Organization's Framework Convention on Tobacco Control opened for ratification by nations who become signatories to it. The USA signed the WHO's Framework Convention on Tobacco Control in 2004 (UN, 2015). Joining USA and Australia were 166 other nations who signed the Framework Convention on Tobacco Control between its opening in May 2003 and its closing on June 29, 2004, though its ratification by additional nations since then brings the total to 180 (WHO FCTC, 2015). Nations can still join today, through a one-step process of ratification.

The recent Australian policies continue a trend of increasing federal restrictions on tobacco advertising in Australia. Australia began with a ban on TV and radio tobacco ads in 1976, continuing with a ban on tobacco sponsorship of sporting events in 1992 (Kennedy, 2012). But with the advent of the Framework Convention on Tobacco Control, even more push for tobacco control has come from the Australian federal government.

In 2011, the Cancer Council of Australia provided research which "suggested that packaging plays an important part in encouraging young people to try cigarettes" (Kennedy, 2012). The Australian government calculated 15,000 Australian smokers died annually at a cost of AU$30 billion (ibid, 2012). Bolstered by these reports, Attorney-General Nicola Roxon introduced plain packaging legislation during her service as Health Minister, backed by strong advocacy from health groups like the Australian Medical Association (Hambleton, 2012, p. 199). The plain packaging policies, with such strong federal support, became law in 2011 and began sweeping the states in 2012. But soon enough, resistance from multinational tobacco companies began at the national level, spreading quickly into litigation and arbitration affecting many nations around the world.

III. Resistance to Australia's Plain Packaging Laws.

National Resistance. British American Tobacco Australia, Japan Tobacco International, Philip Morris, and Imperial Tobacco Australia challenged the plain packaging policy in the Australian High Court (ibid, p.199). These companies argued "the new measures amounted to the acquisition of their brands by the Government without just compensation, and should be ruled unconstitutional." But, while the High Court admitted the policy "regulated the plaintiffs' intellectual property rights and imposed controls," the Commonwealth of Australia gained no "proprietary benefit or interest" from them (ibid, p. 199). The court ruled the new laws constitutional.

The *American Journal of Law & Medicine* explained the judicial response to the tobacco company claims of trademark infringement. It is worth considering the legal reasoning in the High Court's ruling on the constitutionality of the plain packaging laws, because Philip Morris International will be objecting to the World Trade Organization with similar intellectual property arguments. The High Court heard arguments which hinged on the "bedrock principle" which defines acquisition, and reviewed whether or not the Commonwealth of Australia had acquired (as legally defined) anything in the process of regulating cigarette packaging. Australian law holds that no acquisition of property takes place without the acquiring party gaining an interest in the property, "however slight or insubstantial" that interest may be (Liberman, 2013, p. 370). The resulting legal arguments focused on whether or not the Commonwealth had acquired any interest in the intellectual property (trademarks) and the property (the packages) of the tobacco companies in the new packaging.

Tobacco lawyers claimed many interests gained by the Commonwealth, such as free advertising for Quitline now that the smoking cessation hotline's number must appear on all cigarette packs (ibid, p. 371). The High Court did not acknowledge any of the interest claims and granted the tobacco companies nothing.

In fact, the High Court used none of the many arguments it had proposed in a preliminary document, arguments in favor of the public health benefits of plain packaging, the government's power to restrict intellectual property rights in the service of the greater public good, and the obligations Australia has now as part of the Framework Convention on Tobacco Control (ibid, p. 377-9). Instead, The High Court ruled the government had gained no interest in the intellectual property, specifically the brands and trademarks of the tobacco companies, and therefore could regulate their packaging as they liked. Case closed.

The simplicity of the High Court's rejection of the claims may or may not foreshadow impending decisions from the World Trade Organization. But they do shine a spotlight on the battle for supremacy between public health and intellectual property rights in courts. Much like the Australian Federal Court's recent ruling on patenting human DNA sequences in *Myriad Genetics*, decisions may hinge on interpreting the legal definition of a phrase or even a single word. In *Myriad*, the phrases were "artificially created state of affairs" and "matter of manufacture" (D'arcy, 2014). Here, the word in question was acquisition. One might expect that, as the court did in their preliminary documents, cases affecting public health will depend on evaluating the benefits they provide to people. But in reality, the argument over the definition of a single word can mark the turning point in who wins: public health policy as envisioned by the World Health

Organization or the corporate intellectual property rights enshrined in the World Trade Organization.

International Resistance. In today's globalized political environment, the legal questions do not end at the federal level. Australia's ruling has resulted in litigation at the international level. Tobacco-exporting nations the Dominican Republic, Ukraine, and Honduras have challenged the plain packaging laws through disputes registered with the World Trade Organization (Hambleton, 2012, p. 199). Ukraine's involvement in the dispute may seem odd, because it does not currently export tobacco into Australia (Morran, 2015). Why does Ukraine suddenly care about the Australian market?

Philip Morris International, one of the defeated plaintiffs in the Australian High Court, has had operations in Ukraine since 1994 when it "acquired a majority share of the JSC Kharkiv tobacco factory. In 1996 the factory started manufacturing the first international PMI brands in Ukraine: *Chesterfield* and *Bond Street*. In 2000, the factory began producing *Marlboro*" (PMI, 2015). Philip Morris International created the Philip Morris Ukraine entity which in March 2013 joined the US-Ukraine Business Council (USUBC), a group of "over 200 companies and organizations" with business and investment interest in Ukraine, including "five other Fortune 500 type companies: Amway, DuPont, Ecolab, Intel, and Visa" (USUBC, 2013). With fourteen regional offices and 1400 employees, Philip Morris Ukraine has a significant interest in keeping Ukrainian tobacco exports financially viable.

Begun in 2012, the Ukrainian dispute, numbered by the World Trade Organization as Dispute DS434, has not reached a conclusion. A panel requested by Ukraine formed in May 2014. In October 2014, the panel announced it would issue a final report "not before the first half of 2016" (WTO, 2014). Ukraine's dispute pits Australia's Tobacco Plain Packaging Act against specific articles of the TRIPS agreement and two other trade agreements: first, GATT, the General Agreement on Tariffs and Trade, with its original 1947 provisions still in effect as modified under the World Trade Organization which replaced it in 1994; and second, the international treaty called the Agreement on Technical Barriers to Trade (or more simply, TBT Agreement) which also coincides with the 1994 creation of the World Trade Organization and became effective in 1995 (WTO, 2014).

Philip Morris has even more fronts where it fights its private war for rights to sell an addictive and dangerous product. Reports in the press accuse Philip Morris International of "shifting control of its Australian cigarette operations to Hong Kong-based Philip Morris Asia" for the express purpose of, less than a year later, suing "the Australian government through an international court, saying the government's plan to force all cigarettes into plain non-branded packaging violated a decades-old trade agreement with Hong Kong" (Morran, 2015). In response, Philip Morris International openly confirms their position that "Australia's plain packaging policy is an unprecedented destruction of brands and breaches Australia's treaty with Hong Kong" (PMI, 2014). The Hong Kong question is one of two Investor State Dispute Settlements now in arbitration and publicly defended in statements by Philip Morris International. The other involves Uruguay.

Uruguay joined the numerous national parties now requesting a consultation on Australia's laws from the World Trade Organization in DS434 (WTO, 2014). But Uruguay's problems with Philip Morris pre-date Australia's plain packaging laws. Philip Morris International dragged Uruguay into arbitration in 2010, claiming that Investor State Dispute Settlement (ISDS) provisions of international trade agreements protected their intellectual property in the forms of branded packaging with trademarks (PMI, 2014). Philip Morris International's public statement on its ISDS cases against Australia (via Hong Kong) and Uruguay are "about governments destroying our... intellectual property. In doing so, both governments violated their pledge under binding international treaties not to deprive investors of their property without fair compensation in return" (PMI, 2014).

Uruguay developed its own policy about graphic warnings on cigarette packages, mandating coverage of 80 percent of the entire package with these warnings. But in addition to this policy which is even more aggressive than Australia's, Uruguay introduced a "ban on selling more than one variant of each cigarette brand," thus preventing Philip Morris from offering a wide range of their brands. And this measure, claims Philip Morris, "violates Uruguay's treaty with Switzerland" (PMI, 2014).

In Uruguay, the potential legal victory for Philip Morris would not be changing the laws. It would be a cash payoff. The treaty with Switzerland is the Uruguay-Switzerland Bilateral Investment Treaty (BIT). Philip Morris International claims Uruguay's laws "caused a substantial decrease in sales and a deprivation of intellectual property rights" which entitles PMI to compensation under the treaty (Sahin, 2014). If Australia's High Court has dashed Philip Morris International's hopes of regaining branded packaging, the company remains steadfastly determined to bilk entire nations for payments to compensate for its reduced sales. After their utterly unconvincing arguments about intellectual property infringements in the Australian High Court, the Philip Morris legal team may have nothing left to do but salvage as much cash money as possible on the way down.

It may not be entirely wasted effort. Philip Morris International and its subsidiaries have products for sale in 180 countries, a number now exactly equal to the number of nations ratifying the WHO Framework Convention on Tobacco Control (USUBC, 2013). Philip Morris International could easily spend decades as a parasite on the public funds and resources of nation after nation. Philip Morris could easily pay its lawyers to keep wasting the time and resources of international organizations while attempting to keep its cash flow positive and its markets as open to exploitation as possible.

IV. Ethical Considerations of Plain Packaging Laws.

Government Investment in Tobacco Companies. Aside from the litigation and trade disputes from tobacco-producing companies and tobacco-exporting nations, no one in the public voices any strong ethical objections to these laws. Neither academic journals nor the current-events media have tales of citizen groups seeking to reclaim their freedom to enjoy colorful tobacco packaging with interactive advertising promotions and distinctive brands. The only ethical questions from scholars and health advocates involve the consistency of these measures with other government activities.

For example, the Australian government has a "$73 billion Future Fund set up to offset future public servant superannuation liabilities" (Hambleton, 2012, p. 200). These liabilities are merely a type of tax payment made by Australian companies based on their employee's earnings, per the Australian Taxation Office (ATO, 2015). The government makes investments to cover its future tax payments on its employees. What do they invest in? Recently, the fund invested "almost $38 million... in tobacco company shares between December 2010, and February 2012" (Hambleton, 2012, p.200). Clearly, different offices of the same federal government can pursue conflicting policy goals. It would not be surprising to see future guidelines developed by the Conference of Parties to the Framework Convention on Tobacco Control to ensure governments are not investing in the same companies parasitizing them for cash payments through lengthy and costly litigation.

More Regulation, Not Less. Tobacco's well-documented links to disease and death, facts the tobacco industry no longer bothers to deny, make it a cause to which not even avid smokers can enthusiastically rally. Few come out in support of "the multinational cigarette companies that have created a virtual money-printing machine" by using "trademarks to compete on image rather than price." True, "governments, the broader business community, and members of the public" do have concerns about losing the tobacco industry as a source of revenue (Sweanor, 2011, p. 683). From the Australian government's Future Fund to the owners and franchisees of small retail shops, to the peddlers of black market chop-chop, tobacco is a proven source of revenue. But the public wants still more restriction on tobacco, not less.

In the United States, anti-smoking groups such as Action on Smoking & Health have criticized their federal government's level of response to its commitment to the Framework Convention on Tobacco Control, accusing it of "sitting on the sidelines of this historic and vital effort" (ASH, 2012). While the USA has not taken such drastic control of packaging at the federal level, it has made other recent restrictions that are in compliance with the established guidelines of the FCTC, and it has done so despite powerful political lobbies from major tobacco companies with historical power bases in the states. For example, what happened to Camel Lights? Now, they are Camel Blue. Marlboro Lights? Now Marlboro Gold. This shift complies with a Framework Convention on Tobacco Control guideline about not allowing packaging that promotes lighter cigarettes as a potentially healthier or less dangerous option than a "full-flavored" cigarette.

But for the most part, the U.S. federal government seems content to let states take the initiative. Arizona and other states have begun to follow California's lead in banning smoking in public places, with many cities like Boston working to ban even eCigs which contain no tobacco and do not create smoke. It would not be surprising to see American state initiatives similar to Framework Convention on Tobacco Control commitments evolving at their own pace just as Australia's different states adopted their smoking cessation signs at their own pace, and with different severity levels to the warnings.

V. Evaluating Australia's Tobacco Control Measures.

Conference of Parties. Nations who have ratified the Framework Convention on Tobacco Control make up the Conference of Parties. Members of this group evaluate and establish guidelines for tobacco control, including "a set of policy options and recommendations on economically sustainable alternatives to tobacco growing" (WHO FCTC, 2015). To date, the conference has determined eight solid guidelines they believe will further the FCTC's goals, with the full text of each guideline published at http://www.who.int/fctc/guidelines/adopted/en/. Generally, the eight guidelines are:

- Protection of public health policies with respect to tobacco control from commercial and other vested interests of the tobacco industry.
- Price and tax measures to reduce the demand for tobacco.
- Protection from exposure to tobacco smoke.
- Regulation of the contents of tobacco products and regulation of tobacco product disclosures.
- Packaging and labelling of tobacco products.
- Education, communication, training, and public awareness.
- Tobacco advertising, promotion, and sponsorship.
- Demand reduction measures concerning tobacco dependence and cessation.

The Conference of Parties has addressed questions about tobacco as a revenue source from the agricultural and production perspective in addition to the retail and point of sale perspective. Their recent report *Policy Options and Recommendations on Economically*

Sustainable Alternatives to Tobacco Growing attempts to answer the question, "What will farmers grow when tobacco control measures reduce global tobacco demand?" In fact, the report says that time is now, and it calls the need to find income alternatives for farming and processing facilities "urgent" (WHO, 2015).

The Conference of Parties is far, far ahead of the pack in evaluating the global effects of Framework Convention on Tobacco Control measures and plain packaging. The Conference of Parties concludes the efforts are demonstrably working. The Conference of Parties is already collaborating on a solid, workable set of guidelines to minimize economic disruption, reclaim the environment from the harmful effects of tobacco farming, and protect sustainable alternatives from being bullied by the interests of tobacco companies. These are outlined in the principles of the report. The report also recommends educational and training programs to be developed after study of community groups by gender, age, education, and ethnicity to help target the programs to them. At the level of the World Health Organization, the contentious twentieth-century debates about potential harm to health and environment from the tobacco industry have been settled long ago. Their only question is, "What next?"

Joint Efforts at the National Level. This forward-thinking attitude of the Conference of Parties is consistent with other published research on plain packaging laws and related tobacco control measures. Evaluations of the plain packaging laws took place before they even began, as research groups sought to predict whether or not they would work in practice. A UK-based research team funded by the Department of Health presented a predictive analysis of whether or not plain packaging would meet the "the guidelines for the International Framework Convention on Tobacco Control: reduced appeal, increased salience and effectiveness of health warnings, and more accurate perceptions of product strength and harm" (Stead, 2013, p.1). By using the FCTC guidelines, the research team reveals the international community's interest in seeing how well Australia's efforts play out on the global stage. This team predicted that plain, dark, standardized packaging would meet all of the FCTC guidelines.

At the national level, the academic community and public health agencies collaborate to evaluate other aspects of tobacco control. For example, research into controlling black market tobacco brought the School of Economics, Finance, and Marketing from RMIT University in Melbourne together with the Center for Population Health, MacFarlane Burnet Institute for Medical Research and Public Health. Working together, these two groups provided empirical evidence about smokers' decisions to smoke chop-chop, a black market form of tobacco which has often been cured and processed outside of the regulatory oversight mandated for legal tobacco production for health reasons. Policy about black market tobacco plays a small but noteworthy role in supporting the broad goal of the plain packaging policy: reducing smoking to less than 10 percent nationally.

The team challenged the prevailing belief that smokers choose chop-chop based on its lower price. The researchers concluded lower price is not the dominant factor in choosing chop-chop over legal tobacco. Instead, their survey suggests availability of black market tobacco was the primary factor in choosing it over legal tobacco. Most former chop-chop smokers now smoking legal tobacco cited lack of availability as their primary motivation for the switch. The researchers concluded with a prediction: Policies aimed at curbing illegal tobacco use through price controls will not be successful, but policies which can reduce the illegal supply will be (Pellegrini, 2011, p. 387).

International Tobacco Control Policy Evaluation Project. National public health departments and university researchers are not the only ones examining Australia from an international guidelines perspective. The International Tobacco Control Policy Evaluation Project exists precisely to study measures like the ones in Australia. Its International Tobacco Control Four Country Survey, or ITC-4, examined one of the supporting measures of Australia's comprehensive polices: point of sale signage warning about tobacco's health risks and posting a smoking cessation hotline in big, bold text. The research team behind the ITC-4 compared mandates about the size, color, text, content, and placement of these signs within various Australian states. The team concluded the anti-smoking signs at retail outlets in Australia correlated to a significant, upward, linear trend in awareness of the signs. The team further correlated this increased awareness with increased interest in quitting smoking, and with increased attempts to do so (Li, 2012, p. 429).

The authors of the study proposed the effectiveness of the signs depends on more than their large size, clear text, simple message, and unmistakable presence in shops. The signs work in tandem with a whole set of policies in different media, and the point of sale warnings are reinforced by the packaging warnings (ibid, p. 430). The researchers also pointed out that individual Australian states had their own timetables for rolling out the signs, with their policies going into effect at different times and with the requirements for the signs varying in intensity from state to state, though strengthened by the less severe states over time (ibid, p. 428).

Though it is too early to have a vast body of published peer-reviewed research on all the long-term effects of plain packaging laws, a wide body of research supports the policies at the academic level, the federal level, and the international level. Australia may soon have data showing whether or not they have reached their stated policy goal of fewer than 10 percent of the population smoking. The most recent statistics on tobacco use from the Australian Department of Health were released in 2014, covering 2013 data. The trend of smoking reduction continues year over year in Australia, down now to 12.8 percent of the population aged 14 or over being daily smokers, and 13.3 percent of people aged 18 or over. These numbers are roughly half the figures from ten years prior (25 percent and 26.1 percent, respectively) (DOH, 2015). Australia's comprehensive efforts and unified federal front have nearly succeeded. Perhaps 2015's data published in 2016 will show they already have.

VI. Conclusion.

Australia has paved the way by acting as a case study for other Framework Convention on Tobacco Control signatory nations. The United Kingdom voted on March 16, 2015 to adopt plain packaging laws similar to Australia's and plans to introduce plain packaging in May 2016 (WHO FCTC, 2015). Ireland voted to implement plain packaging laws early in March, followed shortly by England, with more United Kingdom members announcing they will, too. The widespread majority support for these measures is apparent from the overwhelming parliamentary approval in England where "The House of Commons voted 367 to 113 in favour of packaging which is uniform in shape, size and design, featuring only the brand name and the usual graphic health warnings. The bill passed through the House of Lords without a vote" (Richardson, 2015).

As one public health advocate noted at the inception of Australia's plain packaging policy, "Contextual factors and the lack of opportunity to undertake controlled experiments mean that one can never predict with certainty what the effect will be" (West 2011, p. 681). But now, four years later, the international community has a good idea of the litigation that will follow in federal and international courts. Nations now have an example of the way such litigation will hinge on questions of intellectual property rights defined by international trade agreements. Nations might expect tobacco companies to spend resources pursuing compensation instead of offering outright resistance to infringement as country after country adopts similar measures.

Plain packaging has gained nearly unilateral support from the academic and research communities, public health agencies, politicians and federal officials, advocacy groups, the medical community, the 180 signatory nations to the Framework Convention on Tobacco Control, and the highest courts in the land. The only serious objectors to plain packaging and other FCTC-based measures to control tobacco remain the companies which profit from tobacco sales, and nations exporting it for sale, especially those where said companies have significant overseas operations despite their origins as U.S.-based corporations. Australia has successfully implemented these policies on a widespread basis with cooperation from its states. Australia has successfully prevented, so far, its public funds from being parasitized by compensatory payments to multinational tobacco companies.

All of this bodes well for other nations seeking similar policy measures to achieve a statistical reduction in tobacco use, leaving the tobacco companies with little recourse but to go to the World Trade Organization. By the end of 2016, the signatory nations of the Framework Convention on Tobacco Control will know whether or not the WTO will favor public health over intellectual property rights, and just what form that legal reasoning will take. The World Trade Organization's position on tobacco control through packaging restrictions on brand and trademark usage will set yet another precedent in the ongoing political power struggle between corporate profit interests and people's health on an international level.

References

Action on Smoking & Health (ASH). (August 7, 2012). "ASH calls on President Obama to immediately submit FCTC for ratification, 8 years after U.S. signed agreement." https://ash.org/ash-calls-on-public-to-urge-obama-senate-to-ratify-whos-framework-convention-on-tobacco-control/#sthash.jHPoeTat.dpuf

Australian Government, Department of Health. (May 6, 2015). "Tobacco key facts and figures: National Drug Strategy Household Survey detailed report 2013." http://www.health.gov.au/internet/main/publishing.nsf/Content/tobacco-kff

Australian Tax Office. (2015). "Superannuation payments." https://www.ato.gov.au/Business/Employers/Payments-and-reporting/Superannuation-payments/

D'Arcy v. Myriad Genetics Inc [2014] FCAFC 115 (2014, September 5). *Federal Court of Australia.* http://www.austlii.edu.au/au/cases/cth/FCAFC/2014/115.html

Hambleton, Steve. (November 2012). "World-leading plain packaging laws squeeze big tobacco." *World Medical Journal*, 58(5/6): 199-200.

Kennedy, Duncan. (Dec. 1, 2012). "Australian smokers given plain packs." *BBC News Sydney.* http://www.bbc.com/news/world-asia-20559585

Li, Lin, et. al. (Feb. 2012). "The association between exposure to point-of-sale anti-smoking warnings and smokers' interest in quitting and quit attempts:

findings from the International Tobacco Control Four Country Survey." *Addiction, 107*(2): 425-433. DOI: 10.1111/j.1360-0443.2011.03668.x

Liberman, Jonathan. (2013). "Plainly constitutional: the upholding of plain tobacco packaging by the high court of Australia." *American Journal of Law & Medicine, 39*(2/3): 361-381.

Morran, Chris. (February 16, 2015). "Meet the new Marlboro spokesman: Jeff, the diseased lung in a cowboy hat." *Consumerist.* http://consumerist.com/2015/02/16/meet-the-new-marlboro-spokesman-jeff-the-diseased-lung-in-a-cowboy-hat/

Pellegrini, Breanna, et. al. (Oct. 2011). "Understanding the motivations of contraband tobacco smokers." *Drugs: Education, Prevention & Policy, 18*(5): 387-392. DOI: 10.3109/09687637.2011.562935. http://www.researchgate.net/profile/Breanna_Pellegrini/publication/232057905_Understanding_the_motivations_of_contraband_tobacco_smokers/links/0c960519d87d815102000000.pdf

Philip Morris International (PMI). (October 13, 2014). "Trade agreements and ISDS: protecting public interest and investors." http://justthefacts.pmi.com/international-trade-agreements-and-isds-protecting-the-intellectual-property-rights-of-legal-business/

Philip Morris International (PMI). (2015). "Country overview: Ukraine."

http://www.pmi.com/marketpages/Pages/market_en_ua.aspx#

Richardson, Hayley. (March 16, 2015). "UK passes law to require plain cigarette packaging in England." *Newsweek.* http://europe.newsweek.com/uk-passes-law-require-plain-cigarette-packaging-england-314110

Sahin, Aylin A. (November 7, 2014). "Philip Morris vs. Uruguay: intellectual property debate in international investment arbitration." *Berkeley Technology Law Journal.* http://btlj.org/2014/11/philip-morris-vs-uruguay-intellectual-property-debate-in-international-investment-arbitration/

Stead, Martine et. al. (October 2013). "Is consumer response to plain/standardised tobacco packaging consistent with Framework Convention on Tobacco Control guidelines? A Systematic Review of Quantitative Studies." *PLoS ONE, 8*(10): 1-10. DOI: 10.1371/journal.pone.0075919

Sweanor, David T. (Nov. 2011). "Effective beats dramatic: A commentary on Australia's plain packaging of cigarettes." *Drug & Alcohol Review, 30*(6): 683-684. DOI: 10.1111/j.1465-3362.2011.00370.x

United Nations (UN). (2015) Status as at 10-05-2015 06:48:08 EDT. *United Nation Treaty Collection.* https://treaties.un.org/pages/ViewDetails.aspx?src=TREATY&mtdsg_no=IX-4&chapter=9&lang=en

US-Ukraine Business Council (USUBC). (March 11, 2013). "Philip Morris Ukraine joins U.S.-Ukraine Business Council (USUBC)."

http://www.usubc.org/site/member-news/philip-morris-ukraine-joins-u-s-ukraine-business-council-usubc

West, Robert. (Nov. 2011). "Preventing tobacco companies from advertising using their packaging could be an important component of comprehensive tobacco control: A commentary on Australia's plain packaging of cigarettes." *Drug & Alcohol Review*, 30(6): 681-682. DOI: 10.1111/j.1465-3362.2011.00369.x

World Health Organization (WHO). (2015). "Guidelines and policy options and recommendations for implementation of the WHO FCTC." http://www.who.int/fctc/guidelines/adopted/en/

World Health Organization (WHO). (2015) "Policy options and recommendations on economically sustainable alternatives to tobacco growing (in relation to articles 17 and 18 of the WHO FCTC)." http://www.who.int/fctc/guidelines/adopted/Policy_options_reccommendations_Articles17_18_COP6.pdf

WHO Framework on Tobacco Control (WHO FCTC). (2015). "Global domino effect in implementing plain packaging." (Announcement on UK vote on plain packaging). http://www.who.int/fctc/en/

World Trade Organization (WTO). (October 30, 2014). "Dispute Settlement: Dispute DS434: Australia: certain measures concerning trademarks and other plain packaging requirements applicable to tobacco products and packaging." https://www.wto.org/english/tratop_e/dispu_e/cases_e/ds434_e.htm

Policy Alternatives to Water Fluoridation

I. Introduction.

In recent interviews, former Minnesota governor Jesse Ventura has advocated an end to adding fluoride to municipal water supplies. He has claimed the Nazis used fluoride in drinking water to pacify people (Isquith, 2014). Ventura has claimed that fluoride is an ingredient in Prozac, and the USA has been effectively dosing its citizens with mood-altering chemicals. Is there any truth to Ventura's confrontational statements about fluoridation? Jay Lehr, author of *The Fluoride Wars*, told interviewers from a Florida newspaper, "The World War II death camp statement is an absurd lie" (Bowers, 2011). But one can easily look up the chemical composition of Prozac and verify it contains fluorine atoms.

For every refuted claim about fluoridation, a new one seems to appear. Paul Connett, PhD, executive director of the Fluoride Action Network, published fifty reasons to oppose in fluoridation in 2004. He continues to present his arguments to municipalities like Dallas, TX, where the January 2015 renewal of a fluoridation contract recently reopened the fluoride debate (Activists, 2014). Connett's reasons range from the cumulative effects of fluoride as a poison, to questioning some studies which link fluoride to decreased rates of tooth decay (Connett, 2004, p. 70-74).

In this atmosphere of conflicting claims and seemingly contradictory information, fluoridation remains a contentious public health policy in the twenty-first century. Both peer-reviewed research and celebrity claims ride a rising tide of public inquiry into the long-accepted practice of fluoridation. The first controlled municipal water fluoridation trial began in 1945 in the USA (Lennon,

2006, p. 759). But 70 years later, citizens continue to argue its merits in city councils and on public ballots across the country. This paper will look at some of those cities.

This paper will also establish, in plain language, facts agreed upon by both sides of the debate, and propose alternative policy measures which simultaneously meet the needs of fluoride supporters and objectors alike. It will give examples of current fluoridation policies in well-known cities, review the claims about health risks and benefits, and provide a clear explanation of what fluoridation really means in chemical terms. The political realities of changing a fluoride policy require not just cooperation between city councils and their constituents, but between two groups with apparently conflicting public health concerns: one concerned about tooth decay, and one concerned about drinking a toxic chemical. That both of these groups seek to advance the cause of public health provides an opportunity for them to collaborate and bring mutually agreeable, politically feasible policies to a public referendum.

II. Who Decides to Fluoridate a City's Water?

If citizens feel concerned the government is fluoridating their water, they first need clarity about which government is involved. The federal government does have a role in setting limits of fluoride in water systems, but the decision to fluoridate comes from municipal governments in most states, and from the state government in a minority of states.

The Federal Government's Role. The federal government does not set fluoridation policy, though federal agencies offer recommendations, and the Environmental Protection Agency (EPA) mandates an upper limit to fluoride content. In April 2015, the US Department of Health & Human Services (HHS) issued a new recommendation for the optimum level of fluoridation, now set at 0.7 milligrams per liter of water. This represents the lower limit of their previous range of 0.7–1.2 mg/L, a range unchanged since HHS issued it in 1962 (HHS, 2015).

This new recommendation is not a mandate to states and municipalities. However, in cities like Boulder, CO, a resulting review of current policy is already underway, including obtaining non-binding recommendations from state governmental agencies like the Colorado Department of Public Health and Environment (Linenfelser, 2015). Boulder's Water Quality Manager explained the review will include an evaluation of whether or not adjusting the fluoridation process to the new target level would still meet the intent of the existing policy.

For some cities, the new federal recommendation has given administrators an opportunity to review policy, but their fluoridation levels are already close to the target. For example, a 1993 census of fluoride levels in Arizona showed Phoenix targeting an optimum level of 0.7 mg/L (HHS, 1993, p. 47). The city's annual water analysis for 2014 shows a minimum fluoride level of 0.5 mg/L and a maximum level of 0.8 mg/L, with average levels at 0.6 mg/L (City of Phoenix, 2014, p.2). This annual analysis by the Water Services Department tests levels at approximately twenty-two different sites (Espericueta, 2015). Phoenix is already very close to its historical target and the new HHS recommendation.

Federal mandate on fluoride comes from the Environmental Protection Agency. The EPA sets a legal cap on the amount of fluoride in public water systems, a cap called the Maximum Contaminant Level (MCL). This cap is public knowledge and appears on the EPA's website about fluoride in drinking water as 4 mg/L. The EPA also sets a secondary level at 2 mg/L, a level intended to prevent a well-documented discoloration in children's teeth which results from excessive fluoride. This secondary level is not mandated, but the EPA does require public water systems to notify them when average levels exceed this threshold (EPA, 2011). *Note:* The measurements of milligrams per liter convert directly to a "parts per million" figure. 4 mg/L equals 4 ppm (EPA, 2015).

Decisions at the Municipal Level. Aside from the federally mandated Maximum Contaminant Level, the decision to fluoridate remains a city or county decision in most states. A minority of states mandate fluoridation for the entire state, and the laws vary somewhat in establishing the minimum size of communities covered by the mandate, and also in their requirements for a public referendum to approve fluoridation (Juneau, 2006, p. 98-101). Therefore, in most U.S. cities, control of fluoridation rests in the hands of voters at the municipal level, and in fewer cases at the state level.

However, it is not always as simple as taking a vote. In Boulder, CO, for example, voters in 2006 had an opportunity to reconsider the fluoridation policy begun in 1969. A ballot initiative gained enough signatures to put fluoride to a public vote. A majority of voters decided to continue fluoridating Boulder's water, though the city's Water Quality Manager reports the measure was only "barely defeated" (Linenfelser, 2015).

A public referendum does not always happen. In 2012, a sub-committee of the city council in Phoenix, AZ addressed concerns about fluoridation. The question of fluoridation was not a ballot initiative in this case, but a matter brought before the city council due to one citizen's concerns about her hypothyroidism (Forsythe, 2012). A council sub-committee heard testimony from chemistry professors, dentists, and public health administrators, but no vote was held. The council sub-committee members agreed to continue the fluoridation policy without taking a vote and without bringing the matter before the full city council for review (Gardiner, 2012). The matter of fluoridation was settled by only a sub-committee of a city council.

Local politics clearly play a role in these decisions. Furthermore, a city council does not always agree with the public when fluoridation is put on the ballot. For example, the city council of Portland, OR voted in 2012 to begin fluoridation, only to have voters refuse fluoridation on the ballot the following May (Innes, 2014).

In some cases, local implementation faces not political challenges but practical ones. In Tucson, AZ, local dentists persuaded their mayor and city council to begin fluoridation in 1992, without resorting to a ballot initiative. But more than two decades later, the fluoridation has not begun. The "first attempt to deliver the water was disastrous, and Tucson Water scrapped a single-point facility, which was part of the original fluoridation plan" (ibid, 2014). A plan to begin fluoridation includes constructing the facility and obtaining equipment to do the job, and this requires planning and budget considerations as well as architectural ones.

Therefore, the decision to fluoridate municipal water systems falls partly to municipal governments, including their administrators, and partly to voters, with voters having recourse to ballot initiatives if they disagree with city council. Regardless of mandate, the logistical and infrastructure realities of a community can determine whether or not the city can truly take action. One would also expect this to hold true even in the minority of states mandating fluoridation from the state level.

III. The Chemicals Used in Fluoridation.

Questions over the toxicity of fluoride must address the specific chemicals used to add it to water systems. The EPA's Maximum Contaminant Level concerns fluoride specifically. But fluoride, a negatively charged ion of the element fluorine, is never added directly to public water systems in the fluoridation process. To fluoridate water, cities choose to use one of three chemicals: sodium fluoride, hydrofluorosilicic acid, and sodium fluorosilicate. (Sodium fluorosilicate, Na_2SiF_6, is also known as sodium silicofluoride or disodium hexafluorosilicate. Hydrofluorosilicic acid, H_2SiF_6, is also called fluorosilicic acid, or HFS, or FSA in the literature.) Each of these three chemicals has a Material Data Safety Sheet, a document well-known to American workers as required for all hazardous substances in workplaces, per the Occupational Safety & Health Administration (OSHA).

Sodium Fluoride. Sodium fluoride is the active ingredient in over-the-counter fluoride mouthwash. The ingredients label on a bottle of ACT Anticavity Fluoride Rinse, for example, shows an active ingredient of 0.05% sodium fluoride (ACT, 2015). Per the instructions on the bottle, anticavity mouth rinses are meant to be held in the mouth for a minute and spit out, never swallowed.

Is sodium fluoride toxic? The Material Data Safety Sheet says yes. The MSDS for sodium fluoride warns of irritant and corrosive effects to eyes and skin, that it "may be toxic to kidneys, lungs, the nervous system, heart, gastrointestinal tract, cardiovascular system, bones, teeth", that "repeated or prolonged exposure" can cause organ damage, and that "severe over-exposure can result in death" (ScienceLab, 2015). The MSDS continues with warnings to not ingest it or breathe its dust in solid form, and specifically says to "prevent entry into sewers." The chemical is slightly explosive in the presence of heat.

Sodium Fluorosilicate. The MSDS for sodium fluorosilicate (sodium silicofluoride) reads similarly to that of sodium fluoride. It notes the irritant and corrosive effects to eyes and skin, warns against breathing the dust, and mentions repeated exposure may cause the chemical to accumulate in the organs, leading to a "general deterioration" in health. The MSDS includes a warning to "prevent entry into sewers," as well as a warning to "never add water to this product" (ScienceLab, 2015). These warnings seem almost intentionally ironic, considering the chemicals are purchased to be added to the water supply system.

Hydrofluorosilicic Acid. Hydrofluorosilicic acid is a byproduct of phosphate production, specifically phosphate-based fertilizer production. The anti-fluoride website FluorideAlert.org claims the acid is a hazardous waste mostly fertilizer production in Florida (Fluoride Action Network, 2015). Finding facts to prove this statement turns out to be surprisingly easy.

For example, the city of Boulder, CO, uses hydrofluorosilicic acid in its fluoridation program (Boulder, 2015). In a phone interview, Boulder's Water Quality Manager pulled a recent invoice from the supplier for this chemical. The acid comes from a chemical company in Florida called Mosaic (Linenfelser, 2015). Mosaic's web page about hydrofluorosilicic acid confirms it is:

> "produced during the concentration of **phosphoric acid** in an evaporation process unique to the **phosphate industry**. The vapor stream from the phosphoric acid reaction is scrubbed with water to form [hydrofluorosilicic acid] from the naturally

occurring silica and fluorine in the phosphoric acid." (Mosaic, 2015).

The Mosaic chemical company includes Mosaic CropNutrition, a fertilizer company. The link between hazardous waste from fertilizer manufacturers and the chemicals used in fluoridation is not a hoax, a scare tactic, or a conspiracy theory. It is an easily verifiable fact. When this fact was brought up in a phone interview with the Chief Water Quality Inspector of the City of Phoenix, he simply agreed (Espericueta, 2015). While the general public may find this connection between fertilizer, hazardous waste, and fluoridation startling or even sinister, public administrators involved in fluoridation are well aware of it and make no attempt to deny it. Safe or not, fluoridation is not a cover-up.

The Material Data Safety Sheet provided on Mosaic's page confirms hydrofluorosilicic acid's toxicity. Like the other two chemicals, it is "corrosive to the skin, eyes, and mucous membranes through direct contact, inhalation, or ingestion." The MSDS warns "overexposure may lead to coma or death." It says, "prolonged or repeated exposure to fluoride compounds may cause fluorosis," a condition characterized not only by discolored tooth enamel but by hardening or softening of bones, joint pain, and limited range of motion (Mosaic, 2015). And like the other two chemicals, users are explicitly warned to "prevent discharge into waterways and sewers."

Therefore, claims that water fluoridation puts hazardous waste into public water are partially correct. Sodium fluoride would not be considered a waste product, but its toxicity and hazardous nature are plainly stated on the Material Data Safety Sheet. Hydrofluorosilicic acid is indeed a reclaimed waste from the fertilizer industry, with a clearly documented toxicity and hazardous nature.

Sodium fluorosilicate is produced by taking that hydrofluorosilicic acid and neutralizing it with sodium carbonate to produce a solid matter, making it merely one more step removed from its origin as hazardous waste (BFS, 2015).

To summarize so far, the EPA has determined any fluoride concentration above 4 mg/L to be unsafe for consumption and illegal. To reach the historical target range of 0.7–1.2 mg/L recommended for dental health by the HHS, cities must add fluoride-containing chemicals, not pure fluoride. These chemicals are known to be toxic and hazardous, and described as such on their OSHA-mandated Material Safety Data Sheets. The decision to add these chemicals is made on the local and municipal level in most states, and occasionally at the state level. Voters have recourse to public ballot initiatives whether they want to begin or end the addition of these chemicals to their water systems.

IV. What Does It Cost to Fluoridate?

Setting aside the one-time costs of installing a new fluoridation system, the ongoing costs depend on several things. A city's population and water usage determine the volume of its water system, which determines the amount of chemicals needed to reach the target level of fluoridation. The natural level of fluoride in local water also affects how much chemical needs to go in the water to reach the HHS target level. The city pays both the cost of the chemicals and the cost of infrastructure (maintenance, labor, testing) to administer them. Public policy debates over fluoridation compare these costs to the reduction in individual costs to treat tooth decay and the related health problems it causes. Federal sources claim the cost of fluoridation on a per-citizen or per-household basis is offset by preventing far greater costs for care.

Example Fluoridation Costs for Three Cities. The city of Boulder, CO shows on its public fluoridation web page an annual cost of $60,000 to buy hydrofluorosilicic acid (Boulder, 2015). Boulder calculates this cost at approximately 85 cents per household annually. A decision to use a different chemical would affect the cost:

> "There are other options and methods that vary in cost due to pureness of grade, availability, and form (powder or liquid). The preliminary cost estimates to purchase the additive for these options vary from about $25,800 annually to over $1.3 million annually. Some options would require additional capital costs to enable city equipment to use the new product and for employees to safely handle the additive" (Boulder, 2015).

Costs for Dallas, TX are somewhat greater. The Dallas City Council recently reviewed a three-year, $1,060,800 contract for fluoridation expiring in January 2015 (Mercola, 2014). *The Dallas Morning News* reported in January the city council voted to continue the contract, with two council members opposed. The beneficiary of this contract is Mosaic CropNutrition (Wilonsky, 2015). Mosaic CropNutrition is a company of Mosaic, Boulder's supplier of hydrofluorosilicic acid, and it is a fertilizer company (Mosaic CropNutrition, 2015).

As of 2012, Phoenix, AZ, spends $420,000 per year for its fluoridation chemicals, part of the total annual cost of $582,000 to fluoridate the water system (City of Phoenix, 2012). Phoenix uses hydrofluorosilicic acid, like Boulder and Dallas, but has a contract with Thatcher Company for the product (Espericueta, 2015). Thatcher Group is a chemical manufacturer and distributor in Utah with a public website at Tchem.com. Thatcher is a supplier of fertilizer products, listed on their site, including the phosphoric acid from which hydrofluorosilicic acid comes (Thatcher, 2015.)

Indirect Cost Reduction to Citizens. The justification of these costs is the simultaneous reduction in health care costs for a city's citizens. A pamphlet made publicly available through a joint effort between the American Dental Association and the Centers for Disease Control claims "for most cities, every $1 invested in community water fluoridation saves $38 in dental treatment costs" and suggests that fluoridation means lower taxes and lower health insurance premiums for the general public (CDC, 2006). The CDC bases these figures, adjusted for current dollar value, on a 2001 economic analysis of fluoridation published in the *Journal of Public Health Dentistry* (CDC, 2015). This analysis determined "the annual per-person cost savings resulting from fluoridation ranged from $15.95 in very small communities to $18.62 in large communities" (Griffin, 2001). The CDC explains:

The analysis takes into account the costs of installing and maintaining necessary equipment and operating water plants, the expected effectiveness of fluoridation, estimates of expected cavities in non-fluoridated communities, treatment of cavities, and time lost visiting the dentist for treatment. (CDC, 2015).

V. What Are the Dental Health Benefits of Fluoride?

The consistent ingestion of fluoride has no benefits to the human body in any of the literature either for or against fluoridation, excepting cases where doctors administered high doses as a temporary treatment for specific ailments. Some sources warn of the health risks of ingesting fluoride and others claim ingestion at current municipal levels is safe. But *no one* touts any benefits of repeatedly ingesting fluoride.

The benefits of fluoride come from its lingering presence on teeth. Its contact with the tooth enamel provides the benefits. No dentist will argue this point. It is why mouthwash says to swish it and hold it on your teeth, spit it out, and avoid eating or drinking anything for a time. The benefits of fluoride derive from its presence on your teeth, not from digesting it in your body. Medical literature is clear on this point, and any family dentist can confirm it.

Fluoride versus the Real Cause of Tooth Decay. Tooth decay does not occur simply due to a lack of fluoride in drinking water. Tooth decay happens when sugar interacts with bacteria in the mouth. As the World Health Organization states in the *WHO Guidelines for Drinking-Water Quality*:

"The etiology of dental caries [tooth decay] involves the interplay on the tooth surface between certain oral bacteria and simple sugars (e.g. sucrose) derived from the diet. In the absence of those sugars in foods and drinks, dental caries will not be a public health problem. However where sugar consumption is high or is increasing, dental caries will be or will become a major public health problem unless there is appropriate intervention" (Lennon, 2004, p.1).

Fluoridation, therefore, is a measure designed to compensate for two things: one, a diet high in added sugar and, two, a level of personal dental hygiene inadequate to compensate for the lingering presence of sugar on one's teeth. As the WHO report makes clear, a low-sugar diet would contribute to a reduction in tooth decay. A dental hygiene regimen focused on removing those sugars before bonding with oral bacteria would also reduce tooth decay.

Many dentists speak out in favor of fluoridation because, especially in demographics with low incomes, dental hygiene is not maintained by parents and therefore not by their children. As Tucson dentist and advocate of fluoridation Dr. Philip Mooberry told the *Arizona Daily Star*, "The kids in my practice are decay-free, most of them. Who this affects is kids who don't get in to see the dentist" (Innes, 2014). This would be predominantly children from low-income families. Dentists hope the lack of adequate dental hygiene and regular care will be compensated for by keeping a low level of fluoride in the mouth due to drinking a city's tap water.

Dental Health Benefits of Topical Fluoride Use. The American Academy of Pedodontics published research by a team of dentists in 1982. The study examined reductions in tooth decay using different concentrations of sodium fluoride-based mouthrinse. "The study was conducted in eight Polk County, FL, high schools... where water fluoride level was less than 0.3 ppm," and it compared reduction rates between daily and weekly rinsing, too (Ringleberg, 1982, p. 305). Over a period of two years, students received a rinse in their classrooms, monitored by a teacher.

This simple classroom activity showed significantly reduced rates of tooth decay from both daily and weekly rinses, and from both 0.2% mouthrinse and 0.05%

mouthrinse. (0.05% is the sodium fluoride concentration listed on over-the-counter product ACT Anticavity Fluoride Rinse.) The group with the greatest reduction used 0.05% mouthrinse daily. This easy, daily routine resulted in a difference of 46.2% fewer signs of tooth decay after two years. However, Dr. Ringleberg, the study's leading author and an assistant public health director at the time, noted similar studies in the literature showed "no significant differences between the effect of daily and weekly rinses." He concluded the differences between frequencies of use were "not sufficient to recommend daily rather than weekly doses." Dr. Ringleberg points out this fact for schools and administrators considering a school-based fluoride rinse program, noting "the cost-effectiveness of a weekly rinse is better." In other words, even a single weekly fluoride rinse creates a marked reduction in tooth decay.

VI. What Are the Health Risks of Ingesting Fluoride?

Fluoride and Prozac. Fluoride is a negatively charged ion of the element fluorine. Fluorine is found on our planet in mineral forms where it combines in molecules with other elements, such as the bond between one calcium and two fluorine atoms in fluorite (CaF_2). Fluorine is "never found in a free state in nature, but always in combination with other elements as fluoride compounds" (BFS, 2015). Bonded sets of fluorine atoms do appear in chemicals, such as the group of three fluorine atoms making up part of the fluoxetine molecule ($C_{17}H_{18}F_3NO$). Fluoxetine hydrochloride is better known by its brand name, Prozac, and other branded and generic forms of the chemical sold as a drug. This explains the chemical truth behind claims about fluoride's role as an ingredient in Prozac.

Claims that the chemicals in fluoridation systems have the same mood-altering and serotonin reuptake-inhibiting effects as the chemicals in Prozac, however, have no supporting research. It would be a mistake to assume a single element determines the properties of all the different molecules where it can be found. For example, pure sodium reacts with water by exploding quite powerfully. A potentially fatal force could result from just a handful of pure sodium thrown into water. But when bonded to chlorine, sodium makes a table salt which dissolves peacefully in water. This example should make it clear that fluorine's well-documented presence in Prozac does mean one can assume every substance with fluorine will act like Prozac.

Fluoride and the Thyroid. Although the World Health Organization believes fluoridation is a beneficial public health policy, they do not deny its dangers. Their report on fluoride in drinking water says the "adverse effects... range from mild dental fluorosis [a discoloration of the tooth enamel] to crippling skeletal fluorosis... a significant cause of morbidity in a number of regions around the world" (WHO, 2006). Skeletal fluorosis manifests as increased bone fractures, joint pain, and impaired mobility. Even those who claim fluoridation is safe cannot deny certain levels of exposure to fluoride through ingestion are not safe for humans.

When a citizen concerned about the effect of fluoride on her thyroid brought the matter to city council in Phoenix, she was not alone in this concern. Fluorine's ability to damage the parathyroid glands and lead to hyperparathyroidism is known from examining patients with skeletal fluorosis. As far back as 1973, a *British Medical Journal* article found five patients of twenty with skeletal fluorosis also had "clear evidence of secondary hyperparathyroidism" (Teotia, 1973, p. 637).

On the other hand, symptoms of hyperthyroidism "were completely relieved by administration of fluorine in 6 of 15 patients; tachycardia was stopped and tremor disappeared with four to eight weeks and loss of weight was stopped" in a 1958 Swiss study which administered, orally and by injection, very large doses of fluoride, as high as 20mg in a single dose (Galetti, 1958). The researchers believed the results stemmed from fluoride's ability to inhibit the "thyroid iodide-concentrating mechanism" and this inhibitory effect on the thyroid took place when iodide levels in the blood were low, but not when iodide was plentiful in blood.

Either way, both sides of the fluoride debate can agree that fluoride can affect the thyroid and parathyroid glands. A high dose administered by a medical professional in a clinical setting may effectively treat specific symptoms, but uncontrolled doses can be clearly dangerous. The World Health Organization does not include thyroid concerns in its 2006 publication *Fluoride in Drinking Water*, though it does believe the studies it reviewed show no cause for concern about fluoride in relation to cancer (p. 34), and no cause for concern about damage to reproductive organs (p. 31) or DNA mutation (p. 31).

Dosage. The World Health organization, like the U.S. Department of Health & Human Services, believes their recommended fluoridation levels make ingestion of fluoride safe and, in fact, beneficial due to a reduction in tooth decay. The exposures to levels of fluoride which cause significant harm are greater than the levels recommended for municipalities. The message is clear. Fluoride in large amounts or over long periods of time can be harmful to human health, though citizens may drink it at low concentrations.

Most reports of fluoride damage to the body take place at levels far above the EPA's Maximum Contaminant Level. But to put the EPA's figure of 4 mg/L into perspective, the same MCL applies to bleach. The EPA sets an enforceable level for chlorine, the disinfectant ingredient in bleach, at the same level as fluoride: 4mg/L (EPA, 2015). In other words, the recommended levels of fluoride in city water are just as safe to drink as bleach diluted to the same level. This does not necessarily mean that either chemical is "safe."

VII. Policy Options for Citizens.

Citizens concerned about fluoridation should seek change through public referendum. In areas of state-mandated fluoridation, this may be a greater task than in areas where individual municipalities choose their own fluoridation policy. Fluoridation has far too much popular support currently, not to mention federal support from the CDC and international support from the WHO, to expect a federal initiative to have any political feasibility.

However, the question of whether or not to fluoridate always arrives at city council or on the ballot as an either/or proposition. Either we add the chemicals, or we do not. The concerns of dentists and parent groups are never met with an alternative solution. As Boulder's recent example demonstrates, many voters want to maintain the dental health benefits of fluoridation. A simple repeal of their fluoridation policy offers no new policy in its place. Without an alternative that pleases dentists and parents, the effort to repeal fluoridation with a public referendum can prove wasted effort.

Therefore, the anti-fluoridation movement faces a considerable hurdle which often goes unnoticed amidst the arguments over whether or not fluoride is "safe," or if its benefits are "real." These questions politicize and polarize the discussion. An alternative policy which removed the risks of ingesting fluoride while making its topical benefits widely available, especially to low-income families and citizens, would instead unify the discussion. With this in mind, what policy options could citizens offer as alternatives?

Elements of a Comprehensive Alternative. Dr. Ringelberg's study of daily and weekly fluoride rinses in classrooms provides a model for a policy which could replace fluoridation. A school-based program would reach children without adequate dental care at home, the group which most concerns dentists who advocate fluoridation. A policy targeting only schools in low-income areas would still reach the children of greatest concern and reduce the overall cost of the policy. City funds currently spent on purchasing hazardous chemicals from out-of-state suppliers could be redirected towards a school-based fluoride rinse program. Cities making decisions to begin fluoridation would have even more funding for a program, as they would not bear the costs of constructing and staffing new facilities or purchasing equipment. For a city like Tucson, where infrastructure challenges prevent a fluoridation citizens requested, an alternative program could meet their needs.

Such a program would provide benefits no fluoridation policy offers. The daily or weekly routine of rinsing makes dental hygiene part of children's lives. It builds long-term habits. It raises their awareness that their teeth may be something worth taking extra care of. The programs offer an opportunity to educate about dental hygiene and its importance, through presentations or literature. Informational literature distributed to children and parents as part of the program would raise community awareness. Fluoridating water provides dental benefits but zero education. Fluoridation does not change behavior or move our culture any closer towards healthy dental hygiene habits. Education will.

Purchasing and distributing fluoride mouthwash to schools may appear less cost-effective than buying hydrofluorosilicic acid by the gallon. But a comprehensive public health program involves communities. A school-based rinse program provides an opportunity for retailers to subsidize its costs. A branded mouthwash company might welcome the opportunity to provide its product to schools at a reduced cost or even no cost as an advertising and marketing opportunity. Manufacturers of fluoride toothpastes, toothbrushes, and dental floss would welcome an opportunity to sponsor a daily or weekly dental hygiene program in schools, especially if they could distribute branded promotional items as part of the program. Providing the tools for dental care from program sponsors would especially benefit low-income families and families in crisis.

One city's perfect solution may not be the ideal policy for another city. In a city with few or no low-income residents, an awareness and education campaign may be all that is needed to make fluoridation unnecessary. Where people have the means and the education to adopt a topical fluoride program personally, distribution of fluoride rinses at schools could be an unnecessary expense. Therefore, citizen groups seeking to craft alternative policy should consider the basic elements of a comprehensive strategy, but tailor them to fit the needs of each unique community.

Such a comprehensive policy would involve the most threatened citizens with their communities and schools, open a public dialogue, and provide opportunities for everyone to contribute to positive change. Fluoridation is far from comprehensive, as it is a benefit received passively and without any awareness or behavior change. If anything, fluoridation encourages poor dental hygiene habits by treating citizens as too simple-minded to take care of themselves. School-based rinse programs would bring the same benefits as fluoridation while working to bring about a culture of dental hygiene where further fluoridation would be unnecessary.

No single tactic can comprehensively solve a public health problem like tooth decay, not when the causes are many and the solution which works in one case may not work in another. As other public health programs demonstrate, such as the recent tobacco control and packaging laws in Australia, citizens need information and support at multiple places and multiple times to effect large-scale changes in behavior. As researchers from the International Tobacco Control Project concluded in regards to the effectiveness of campaigns to reduce tobacco smoking in Australia, the policies are effective because they are part of a comprehensive set of policies aimed at multiple media channels and including warnings both at the point of sale and on packaging (Li, 2012, p. 430). Comprehensiveness matters.

Options for Those Who Cannot Stop Fluoridation. In communities where the majority favors fluoridation, policy should make some allowance for those who object. It seems contrary to fundamental American ideals such as liberty and self-determination to force people to accept a known hazardous chemical in their water, regardless of what benefits it may have. An option to buy bottled, purified water is open to anyone who can afford the cost, but it does nothing to address the use of fluoridated water for bathing, hygiene, or cooking, nor the needs of those low-income families who may find the cost a burden.

Fortunately, one state has already come up with a politically feasible and fair policy. According to a 2000 review of fluoridation laws in all 50 states, Georgia "specifies that any person deemed allergic to fluoridated water who finds it necessary, upon advice of a physician or approval of the Department of Human Resources, to buy a defluoridation device may count it as a tax deductible item" (qtd. in Juneau, 2006, p. 98). This policy still places the initial cost of opting out of fluoridation on the individual objector, but it offers a corresponding reduction in tax liability. A tax deduction could easily be extended to any resident who objects to fluoride and wants to install a filtration system to remove it. While Georgia's measure is laudable, it should go farther in offering the deduction to anyone and remove the administrative hurdles of proving an allergy or seeking approval. An objection to drinking toxic chemicals should be sufficient.

A truly egalitarian policy of this nature would include an additional allowance for those who only claim the standard deduction on their income taxes. After all, a tax credit is only good to someone who itemizes their deductions, and the people who do not itemize tend to be lower income people. To avoid placing an undue burden on low-income citizens for opting out of community-mandated fluoride, the tax credit could be made available to all taxpayers regardless of itemizing their deductions or not, much like the Earned Income Credit and other tax credits any tax filer may calculate individually on their return.

VIII. Conclusion.

Anti-fluoridation efforts have failed for two main reasons. First, the number of unsupported claims and wild accusations harm the efforts by exchanging controversy for hard facts. Citizens with legitimate concerns about consuming a hazardous waste product find themselves associated with "tin foil hats" and "conspiracy theories." Second, when the seriousness of their claims becomes a matter of discourse in city councils and public ballots, no alternative policy is provided for concerned dentists and parents. To succeed in removing the toxic chemicals of the fluoridation process from water supplies, anti-fluoride activists need to find a way to provide the topical benefits of fluoride to communities. A school-based program of supervised daily or even weekly fluoride rinses would bring the benefits of fluoride to communities, and it would provide a touch point for other comprehensive measures for education and awareness. If sugar and dental hygiene are the real culprits behind tooth decay, a comprehensive policy would address them directly rather than indirectly through addition of hazardous chemicals to the water supply.

References

ACT. (2015). "ACT Anticavity drug facts."
http://www.actoralcare.com/products/act-anticavity/

Activists for Truth and Liberty. (June 16, 2014). "Dr. Paul
Connett, PhD speaks to Dallas City Council on June 11,
2014." Video https://youtu.be/xguPD85-BH4

Bowers, Becky. (October 6, 2011). "Truth about fluoride
doesn't include Nazi myth." *Politifact Florida (Tampa
Bay Times, Miami Herald).*
http://www.politifact.com/florida/statements/2011/oct
/06/critics-water-fluoridation/truth-about-fluoride-
doesnt-include-nazi-myth/

British Fluoridation Society. (2015). "Technical aspects of
water fluoridation."
http://www.bfsweb.org/facts/tech_aspects/chemsman
ufac.htm

Centers for Disease Control and Prevention (CDC). (2015).
"Cost savings of community water fluoridation."
http://www.cdc.gov/fluoridation/factsheets/cost.htm

Centers for Disease Control and Prevention (CDC) and
American Dental Association (ADA). (2006). "Water
fluoridation: nature's way to prevent tooth decay."
http://www.cdc.gov/fluoridation/pdf/natures_way.pdf

City of Boulder, Colorado. (2015). "Inquire Boulder:
fluoride."
https://user.govoutreach.com/boulder/faq.php?cid=23
302

City of Phoenix Water Services Department. (May 7, 2012). "Q & A fluoride" (listed as Fluoride use in tap water on website). https://www.phoenix.gov/waterservicessite/Document s/wsdfluoride070512b.pdf

City of Phoenix Water Services Department, Environmental Division. (2015). "2014 typical water analysis." PDF retrieved via email to the author from the department.

Connett, Paul. (2004). Fifty reasons to oppose fluoridation. *Medical Veritas, 1*, 70-80. http://www.waterskraus.com/pdf/50%20Reasons%20t o%20Oppose%20Fluoridation.pdf

Environmental Protection Agency (EPA). (2015). "Basic information about fluoride in drinking water." http://water.epa.gov/drink/contaminants/basicinform ation/fluoride.cfm

Environmental Protection Agency (EPA). (2015). "Basic information about disinfectants in drinking water: chloramine, chlorine and chlorine dioxide." http://water.epa.gov/drink/contaminants/basicinform ation/disinfectants.cfm

Environmental Protection Agency (EPA). (January 2011). "Questions and answers on fluoride." http://water.epa.gov/lawsregs/rulesregs/regulatingcon taminants/sixyearreview/upload/2011_Fluoride_Questi onsAnswers.pdf

Espericueta, Pete. (May 7, 2015). *Phone interview with author.*

Forsythe, Jerilyn. (August 16, 2012). "One woman's curiosity reopens water fluoridation debate in Phoenix." *Cronkite News.* http://cronkitenewsonline.com/2012/08/one-womans-curiosity-reopens-water-fluoridation-debate-in-phoenix/

Fluoride Action Network. (2015). "Water fluoridation: fluoridation chemicals." *FluorideAlert.org.* http://fluoridealert.org/issues/water/fluoridation-chemicals/

Galetti, P and Joyet, G. (October 1958). "Effect of fluorine on thyroidal iodine metabolism in hyperthyroidism." *Journal of Clinical Endocrinology & Metabolism, 18*(10), 1102-1110. Reprinted text http://www.slweb.org/galletti.html

Gardiner, Dustin. (September 11, 2012). "Phoenix panel decides to continue fluoridating drinking water." *AZCentral* (The Republic). http://archive.azcentral.com/community/ahwatukee/articles/2012/09/11/20120911phoenix-panel-decides-continue-fluoridating-drinking-water.html

Griffin, S. O., et. al. (Spring, 2001). "An economic evaluation of community water fluoridation." *Journal of Public Health Dentistry, 61*(2), 78-86. Abstract: http://www.ncbi.nlm.nih.gov/pubmed/11474918

Innes, Stephanie. (November 2, 2014). "Cavities again? Blame the Tucson water system." *Tucson.com* (Arizona Daily Star). http://tucson.com/news/science/health-med-fit/cavities-again-blame-the-tucson-water-system/article_33d26ed3-2fb0-5385-b14c-e97630237f4e.html

Isquith, Elias. (December 2, 2014). "These pseudo-religious people who I find laughable: Jesse Ventura talks Republicans, Nazis and running for president." *Salon.* http://www.salon.com/2014/12/02/these_pseudo_religious_people_who_i_find_laughable_jesse_ventura_talks_republicans_nazis_and_running_for_president/

Juneau Fluoride Study Commission. (July 11, 2006). "Report to the Assembly of the City and Borough of Juneau: Exhibit C Summaries of Actions on Fluoridation in Other Jurisdictions." http://fluoridealert.org/wp-content/uploads/juneau.2006.ages94-110_Exhibit_C.pdf

Lennon, Michael A. (September 2004). "Rolling revision of the WHO guidelines for drinking-water quality: fluoride (Draft)." *World Health Organization.* http://www.who.int/water_sanitation_health/dwq/nutfluoride.pdf

Lennon, Michael A. (September 2006). "One in a million: the first community trial of water fluoridation." *Bulletin of the World Health Organization, 84*(9), 759-760. http://www.ncbi.nlm.nih.gov/pmc/articles/PMC2627472/pdf/17128347.pdf

Li, Lin, et. al. (Feb. 2012). "The association between exposure to point-of-sale anti-smoking warnings and smokers' interest in quitting and quit attempts: findings from the International Tobacco Control Four

Country Survey." *Addiction, 107*(2), 425-433. DOI: 10.1111/j.1360-0443.2011.03668.x

Linenfelser, Bret. (May 6, 2015). *Phone interview with author.*

Mercola, Joseph. (July 1, 2014). "Expert testimony: how your drinking water may be damaging your brain." http://articles.mercola.com/sites/articles/archive/2014/07/01/water-supply-fluoridation.aspx#_edn1

Mosaic. (2015). "Hydrofluorosilicic acid (FSA or HFS)." http://www.mosaicco.com/products/industrial_products_hfs.htm

Mosaic. (2015). *Material Safety Data Sheet: hydrofluorosilicic acid.* http://www.mosaicco.com/documents/Hydrofluosilicic_Acid_MSDS_03Jan14.pdf

Mosaic CropNutrition. (2015). *CropNutrition.com.*

Ringleberg, M. L., et. al. (1982). "Effectiveness of different concentrations and frequencies of sodium fluoride mouthrinse." *The American Association of Pedodontics,* 4(4): 305-308. http://www.aapd.org/assets/1/25/Ringelberg-04-04.pdf

ScienceLab. (2015). *Material Safety Data Sheet: sodium fluoride.* http://www.sciencelab.com/msds.php?msdsId=9927595

ScienceLab. (2015). *Material Safety Data Sheet: sodium silicofluoride.*

http://www.sciencelab.com/msds.php?msdsId=992503
7

Teotia, S., et. al. (1973). "Secondary hyperparathyroidism
in patients with endemic skeletal fluorosis." *BMJ, 1,*
637-640.
http://www.ncbi.nlm.nih.gov/pmc/articles/PMC15886
49/pdf/brmedjo1547-0019.pdf

Thatcher Company. (2015). "Thatcher agriculture:
agriculture product list."
http://tchem.com/industries/agriculture/

US Department of Health & Human Services (HHS).
(September,1993.) "Fluoridation census: Arizona."
http://www.fluoridealert.org/wp-
content/uploads/arizona_census.pdf

US Department of Health and Human Services (HHS).
(April 27, 2015). "HHS issues final recommendation for
community water fluoridation: Adjusted level seeks to
maintain dental health benefits of fluoride."
http://www.hhs.gov/news/press/2015pres/04/20150427
a.html

US Department of Health and Human Services (HHS).
(September 2003). "Toxicological profile for fluorides,
hydrogen fluoride, and fluorine."
http://www.atsdr.cdc.gov/toxprofiles/tp11.pdf.
Summary page at
http://www.atsdr.cdc.gov/toxprofiles/tp.asp?id=212&ti
d=38

Wilonsky, Robert. (January 28, 2015). "After year of debate,
Dallas City Council votes not to remove fluoride from

city's water supply." *The Dallas Morning News: City Hall Blog.* http://cityhallblog.dallasnews.com/2015/01/after-year-of-debate-dallas-city-council-votes-not-to-remove-fluoride-from-citys-water-supply.html/

World Health Organization. (2006). *Fluoride in drinking-water* by J. Fawell, et. al. London, UK: IWA Publishing. http://www.who.int/water_sanitation_health/publications/fluoride_drinking_water_full.pdf

World Health Organization (WHO). (2004). "Fluoride in Drinking-water: Background document for development of WHO Guidelines for Drinking-water Quality." http://www.who.int/water_sanitation_health/dwq/chemicals/fluoride.pdf

About the Author

Matthew earned a Bachelor of Interdisciplinary Studies in Public Administration in 2014 from Northern Arizona University. He continues his studies at Fort Hays State University where he is working towards a Master of Liberal Studies in Public Administration. He studies public policy as it relates to patents, international trade agreements, health, and telecommunications in the Internet age. He also holds two degrees from Phoenix College, an Associate in General Business and an Associate in Marketing. He began self-publishing his own work in 2014. In addition to his public policy essays, Matthew has published a book of poetry and drawings, a dream journal, an ongoing science fiction adventure series, and two albums of original guitar music.

Matthew enjoys helping other authors self-publish their work. He supports authors, speakers, and business professionals in creating books that provide positive, practical information to improve people's lives and make a difference in our world. Their recent projects have contributed to greater awareness in the fields of business leadership, interpersonal communication, personal finance, and health & nutrition.

Having studied professional editing, technical writing, and document production management at the university level, Matthew brings many skills to these projects, from editing and interior design to the creation of Kindle-ready documents. He consults on all aspects of the writing and self-publishing process, and supports authors by helping them manage their book projects and production teams.

www.ingramcontent.com/pod-product-compliance
Lightning Source LLC
Chambersburg PA
CBHW060633280326
41933CB00012B/2027